HANDBOOK
FOR HEALING

HANDBOOK FOR HEALING

SIXTEEN WAYS TO FIND BALANCE, CREATE COMPASSION, AND HEAL YOUR HEART

CHRISTY YOUNG

Handbook for Healing:
Sixteen Ways to Find Balance, Create Compassion, and Heal Your Heart
Published by Winged Goddess Media
Richmond, Virginia, U.S.A.

YOUNG, CHRISTY, Author
HANDBOOK FOR HEALING
CHRISTY YOUNG

Library of Congress Control Number: 2024908340

ISBN: 979-8-9899710-0-8, 979-8-9899710-2-2 (paperback)
ISBN: 979-8-9899710-3-9 (hardcover)
ISBN: 979-8-9899710-1-5 (digital)

BODY, MIND & SPIRIT / Healing / Prayer & Spiritual
HEALTH & FITNESS / Mental Health
BIOGRAPHY & AUTOBIOGRAPHY / Artists, Architects, Photographers

Illustrations: Christy Young (christyyoungartist.com)
Editing: Lisa Shrewsberry (getfinelines.weebly.com)
Design: Andrea Reider (reiderbooks.com)
Publishing Management: Susie Schaefer (finishthebookpublishing.com)

QUANTITY PURCHASES: Schools, companies, professional groups, clubs, and other organizations may qualify for special terms when ordering quantities of this title. For information, email info.wingedgoddess@gmail.com.

HANDBOOK FOR HEALING

SIXTEEN WAYS TO FIND BALANCE, CREATE COMPASSION, AND HEAL YOUR HEART

CHRISTY YOUNG

Handbook for Healing:
Sixteen Ways to Find Balance, Create Compassion, and Heal Your Heart
Published by Winged Goddess Media
Richmond, Virginia, U.S.A.

YOUNG, CHRISTY, Author
HANDBOOK FOR HEALING
CHRISTY YOUNG

Library of Congress Control Number: 2024908340

ISBN: 979-8-9899710-0-8, 979-8-9899710-2-2 (paperback)
ISBN: 979-8-9899710-3-9 (hardcover)
ISBN: 979-8-9899710-1-5 (digital)

BODY, MIND & SPIRIT / Healing / Prayer & Spiritual
HEALTH & FITNESS / Mental Health
BIOGRAPHY & AUTOBIOGRAPHY / Artists, Architects, Photographers

Illustrations: Christy Young (christyyoungartist.com)
Editing: Lisa Shrewsberry (getfinelines.weebly.com)
Design: Andrea Reider (reiderbooks.com)
Publishing Management: Susie Schaefer (finishthebookpublishing.com)

QUANTITY PURCHASES: Schools, companies, professional groups, clubs, and other organizations may qualify for special terms when ordering quantities of this title. For information, email info.wingedgoddess@gmail.com.

This book is dedicated to my mother, Katherine,
who taught me the importance of a having
a relationship with God,
the meaning of spirituality,
and the power of prayer.

DISCLAIMER

Please note that this book details the author's personal experiences and opinions, and she makes no representations or warranties of any kind with respect to this book or its contents. The statements made in this book are not intended to diagnose, treat, cure, or prevent any condition or disease. They are meant to assist you in healing and do not replace medical care or therapy.

All content is for informational and educational purposes and does not establish any kind of patient/client relationship. Although we strive to provide accurate information, the information presented here is not a substitute for any kind of professional advice. Please consult with your own physician or healthcare specialist regarding the suggestions and recommendations made in this book. Before you begin any healthcare program, or change your lifestyle in any way, you should consult your physician or another licensed healthcare practitioner to ensure that you are in good health and that the examples contained in this book will not harm you.

Except as specifically stated in this book, neither the author nor the publisher, nor any authors, contributors, or other representatives, will be liable for damages arising out of or in connection with the use of this book.

This is a comprehensive limitation of liability that applies to all damages of any kind, including (without limitation) compensatory; direct, indirect, or consequential damages; loss of data, income, or profit; loss of or damage to property and claims of third parties.

If you are experiencing severe anxiety and depression or an immediate crisis, please reach out to a mental health professional, a crisis center, or a hotline.

TABLE OF CONTENTS

TABLE OF CONTENTS

THE GUEST HOUSE

This being human is a guest house.
Every morning a new arrival.
A joy, a depression, a meanness,
some momentary awareness comes
as an unexpected visitor.
Welcome and entertain them all!
Even if they are a crowd of sorrows,
who violently sweep your house
empty of its furniture,
still, treat each guest honorably.
He may be clearing you out
for some new delight.
The dark thought, the shame, the malice,
meet them at the door laughing
and invite them in.
Be grateful for whatever comes,
because each has been sent
as a guide from beyond.

— Rumi

INTRODUCTION

We are living in flesh and bone and blood bodies here on this Earth, with a mind and an intelligence that are pulling us towards our higher levels, our greatest selves, our highest good. This is for our own soul's growth and expansion as well as for the world at large, for our collective humanity. There is a special place where biology, quantum physics, and spirituality meet in our miraculous selves; we are living, breathing examples of God's handiwork. There is an incredible cosmic intelligence available to us and the study of metaphysics can help to explain some of it. The Oxford Dictionary defines metaphysics as, "The branch of philosophy that deals with the first principles of things, including abstract concepts such as being, knowing, substance, cause, identity, time, and space." While it's impossible to truly quantify its brilliant magnificence, we can feel it in real time, in fleeting, but hopefully not infrequent, rare moments as we embrace the ultimate goal of completely embodying it. There is undoubtedly a God-force, a life-force, within us.

1

We are entering a new and better epoch, leveling up, as it were, entering an era when we can heal, reach a higher vibration, and find the ultimate in catharsis and clarity. And as we are each on different paths with different timing, it is possible to show each other the way. I am here to help direct you back, to remind you of that which you were born to, your true knowing. I have always had a deeper sense that we are not alone on these paths, that we are divinely guided by unseen forces. They can be called angels, deities, or spiritual guides. I, personally, cannot deny this confluence, this miracle, this mysterious presence of God and my experiences with divine intervention. I know that I am led by this divine presence in my life. I am connected to my higher levels, and they guide me through every challenge I've endured; that is truly a comfort, if not what saved me. Therefore, I believe science and spirituality coexist in a beautiful, exquisite universe and you, too, are its living manifested proof.

My first foray into deep relaxation and meditation was a scuba diving class where we had to find something called neutral buoyancy. When you achieve neutral buoyancy, you balance with the gravity that would make you either sink or float. I learned this technique under the deep blue waters of some of the Earth's most beautiful oceans, descending to a quiet place marked by the rhythm of the undulating sea fans and live coral. The sun dappling in and on the reef with its glorious colors was indeed a beautiful sight. For me and the members of my scuba class, achieving buoyancy meant floating and using our breath to control our bodies' movements up or down, our lungs acting as natural buoyancy compensators. Other variables impacting the experience included how much air we had in our tanks, the thickness of our wetsuits, and whether or not we were wearing weight belts. The goal was to achieve a feeling of weightlessness. When you reached the sweet spot of perfect balance, you knew it! There was less of a struggle, and more of a floating, flying feeling. That is what I encourage us all to achieve in life: when things get challenging, find the calm, find the stillness, find your neutral buoyancy.

I have since tried to find something similar in modern life: a deep relaxation, a still point. My scuba days morphed into motherhood days. I had three children, all natural childbirths, all birthed at a maternity center with the support of midwives. The midwives at the Maternity Center in my hometown suggested a course called *HypnoBirthing* by Marie Mongan. It came complete with audio recordings of guided meditations, and I would listen to these meditations daily. Mongan believed in self-hypnosis to achieve a degree of relaxation which could make it possible to experience a painless birth. She believed, as I do, that "a person who is in a hypnotic state is fully awake and even in a heightened state of awareness." (Page 6, *HypnoBirthing, a Celebration of Life* by Marie F. Mongan, M.Ed., M. Hy. Rivertree Publishing 1992, 1998).

I was familiar with meditation at that time as I was a yoga student and enjoyed the practice. I've now been practicing yoga for twenty-five years, and over the years I have come to love its supportive presence in my weekly routine. Birth, of course, is a natural event and not a crisis at all, but Western medicine often tends to treat it like one, and hypnobirthing represented a welcome alternative. With each subsequent pregnancy, I took refreshers in this hypnotherapy technique, just to get my mind back in the game before labor and delivery with my second and third children. These were profound and powerful ignitions for me, as they opened for me the realm of surrendering to that which you cannot control and helped me find my still point when all seemed to intensify as my body and mind dealt with the physical challenges of birth. Although each of my labor and delivery stories was different, I employed the hypnobirthing practices of deep relaxation, guided meditation, and light touch massage during my children's births, and my experiences were all natural, calm, joyous, wonderfully profound, and empowering.

When I pause to consider, I realize this foundation also helped me prepare for what was to come and assisted me in handling crises with calmness.

I understand courses offered in hypnosis are also offered in sports, such as golf. The idea, when applied to sports, is to find the still point to optimize one's best self and skills, to trust, visualize, and surrender to some degree, and to keep any anxieties or fears at bay. This state has also been described as "finding our flow." Mihaly Csikszentmihalyi was a Hungarian American psychologist who is credited with popularizing the term. He described it as "the holistic sensation that people feel when they act with total involvement." When we are in that place, we are in what seems like a timeless zone where we can maximize and access a mind and a genius that is unobstructed by daily distractions and obstacles in life. Our mind is a wonderful, powerful thing.

Why I Wrote This Book

Between 2009 and 2019, I studied and obtained my Reiki I, II, and Reiki Master certifications. This study of hands-on healing led me to start a private practice offering private sessions as well as wellness workshops in a variety of destinations with two longtime friends, both of whom were working hard in their respective fields of yoga, reiki, and meditation, and relationship coaching for trauma and addictions. In 2019, during a moment of reprieve and relaxation while I was sitting on my back porch on a hot summer day, I was both moved to write down ten points which turned into these chapters, the basis of this handbook. It came to me, quite quickly and succinctly, as a download. My healing journey through many hardships in life has prompted me to want to pay it forward, to offer written words with drawings in a handbook-style volume drawn from my own life experiences. What you will find within these pages are simple reminders to the reader and my clients of things we inherently know already, we just need to be guided back to them. I also would love for you to be inspired here, through my own personal accounts within these chapters—to dwell in possibility more, to dream more, to turn things over to a higher power when the burden becomes too much, and to create a clearer channel to allow the messages to flow to you from your guides, who are always there, ready to help you navigate your very own personal and unique journey of life. I would love for you to intensify your faith, to believe that at any point in life we have the power to transmute and transform all our pain and strife into being the greatest and best version of ourselves. It is possible to dream your life into a new way of being! But it does take a dogged determination to want to change, too. Are you ready to join me?

CRISIS, PAIN, AND LOSS

The wound is the place where the light enters you.

—Rumi

In my fifty years on this planet, I have noticed that nobody leaves the planet without having suffered. To experience pain—heartbreak, betrayal, anxiety, futility, fear, shame, sadness, grief, loneliness, and more—is to be human. What's more, I recognize that to know love is to experience loss; they are entwined, and there is no way to have one without the other.

But it's also true that our joys and our pain are rooted in the same soil. Our challenges and adversities can either bring us down or they can be opportunities for us to raise ourselves up, to evolve spiritually and expand and grow into our better selves. Our suffering can bring personal expansion and growth and can bring us to new heights of understanding and compassion, if we choose to say yes to the challenge, if we choose to accept the assignment.

In times of hardship and struggle, we can choose to come out better, not bitter. It has been said that we acquire the strength of that which we overcome and that there is nothing stronger than the human spirit. You, in your beautiful body, mind, and spirit, naturally possess a will to live and the amazing ability to heal, to love, and to flourish. Your struggles and your strengths are completely unique to you, as is the path you are creating for yourself.

No matter what is causing you to feel stuck, disconnected, sorrowful, or full of despair, and no matter what kind of emotional turmoil or pain you are experiencing, you can always start here and now along the path of healing. I encourage you to trust that the healing will come. Though it's true that time does heal, I also believe that part of the process stems from the opportunities we are given to heal and layer love onto and into our wounded heart. It's never too late.

The effort to keep walking forward can require a minute-by-minute or day-by-day focus of attention, and that one small feeling of hope can be a life ring, or even a rescue raft, onto which we can climb. It can help us pivot, and maybe eventually help us head in the direction of a safe space where we can completely relinquish our heavy days and dim thoughts, a space where we can live in the sunshine without fear or pain.

I invite you to consider that feelings of despondency, futility, fear, anxiety, shame, disconnectedness, and sadness are indicators that you are not allowing the Universe to flow into and through your life. This flow is the lifeblood of and the secret to healing! It is important that you just keep going. It is most certainly okay to be angry with God and the Universe for having delivered these circumstances to you. When I was going through my own dark night of the soul, there were many days when I simply did not want to get out of bed. I was so energetically tired that I would wake up after a full night's sleep and still feel exhausted.

It was extremely difficult to muster the energy to keep on going, to put one foot in front of the other. In times like these, we need to look outside of ourselves, to call upon a higher power, and to reach for something greater than ourselves to help us through the day. I remember once, in my darker days, my young daughter asked me what my favorite color was, and I said, "I don't know, I don't have a favorite color today." I was so paralyzed by grief and fatigue that I couldn't even pretend and come up with one single color!

Remember Your Breath

Sometimes it is enough to just remember to breathe. When you get to the end of the day, tell yourself you did the best you could. When all the work and pain seem insurmountable and overwhelming, take a breather, take a break. Then, take action only when your next wave of energy arrives, because it will come—it is already on its way. Remind yourself that at this very moment, the Universe is watching you grow and expand into your greater self.

Sometimes the Universe asks a lot of you—it may seem as though there is just too much to manage, too much heartache and pain, too much of an unbearable loss to digest and process. I know that we can eventually move from hurting, to acceptance, to peace. Our suffering is not for naught; it most certainly is a bridge to compassion.

We can ask God to give us strength, fortitude, and clarity. Know that each day, once lived, is done, and tomorrow is a brand-new day, another chance to get it right. You may never want to relive the day you just experienced, and you may cry every day for a long while. Eventually, however, the clouds will break, and you'll see slivers of sun. Isn't it a relief in some way to know there is a soft pillow and a safe place waiting for your head to rest at night?

One day you will get up and recognize that there is still beauty in the world: a sprouting flower, a small bird, a butterfly, clouds moving across the sky, the magnificent colors of a sunrise or a sunset.

Your life may be altered forever by the experience you've had. There will be pain and suffering from the losses you have endured. But what if they made you stronger, wiser, deeper, more radiant? What if you were to come out the other side a better version of yourself, more appreciative of life, not taking your days, your liberties, for granted? There are no guarantees for any of us, and life is indeed fragile. But that is the very thing that makes it so beautiful, so wondrous, and so precious, too.

Inspiration for Today:

Keep moving forward. Chant a mantra, if you need it, to keep you going:

"I am going to get through this. I will come out of this *better*, not *bitter!*"

SEEKING HOPE

Never give up, for that is just the place
and time the tide will turn.

– Harriet Beecher Stowe

The little book that you have in your hands is intended to give you the hope you seek. It contains the tools that I, myself, used to heal from many traumatic experiences and I still use them today to help me find peace and calm—not just on the surface but at my core. By employing these specific tools—any, or all of them—I know you will find benefits to the overall mind and body, and some relief from the pain and discomfort you may feel. Trust that the healing will come. It always does.

Yet finding hope takes courage. A positive, happy mindset is a hard-earned state, and it is the result of a choice; it requires a conscious decision and a disciplined practice. It involves an active shift in the energetic vibrations we emit. Maintaining a healthy mind and body creates a wall of defense that supports our immune system, buffering us from injury or sickness. So, it's important to strive for this healthy energetic field: our old belief patterns and the oftentimes false and fear-based narratives we create will only deplete us and weaken our defenses, thus leading to future injury and illness. It is good to remember, then, that a healthy body and mind work in unison, and that you are the primary beneficiary.

There are many days in my past that I never want to relive. As I mentioned earlier, I was exhausted, even after a full night's sleep. It was hard to find the energy to keep on going and put one foot in front of the other. If you've been there, too, or if you are there now, why not try to call upon a higher power to help you through the day, or even just the next few hours? Ask for strength and courage as you lead the charge into the unknown.

Sometimes maybe all you can muster is just a small spark of hope, but it is there, like a small flicker of flame on a candle. And, like the element of fire, it can be fanned, and it can grow bigger. When all is falling apart, just find something, *one thing,* to be grateful for; this is essential, and it is what saved me. When I was going through the extremely heavy days of my divorce, this was my turning point. Despite all the turmoil in the world around me, I realized I could always find something to be grateful for, even if the world as I knew it to be—the world I had worked so hard for—was crumbling. I lay in bed one night, thinking "I am grateful my house has heat."

My World Overturned

One summer day when I was fifteen, I came home from a beach vacation with another friend's family to see my parents standing in the driveway, waiting for me.

"Paul died," my father said as the car rolled to a stop.

It was something I couldn't comprehend. My thirteen-year-old brother had been wrestling with ongoing health issues in the hospital since he had been a baby. Now he was gone. I went into shock. I remember what I was wearing, and how I threw a notebook and pen, and my shoes, out of the car door and onto the grass of our front yard when we pulled up before I stepped out. In that very moment, my world turned upside down.

Paul and I had been close all our lives, and I cannot remember a part of my childhood that did not include him. We played many fun, imaginary games and laughed a lot; he brought so much levity into our lives. But he had been in and out of Children's Hospital in Washington, D.C., his whole life. My parents had adopted him when he was only two months old, and they had not been fully informed of some of the serious medical issues from which he suffered. One was a gastrointestinal problem that kept him from keeping food down. He would throw up suddenly at the dinner table at times, almost as a reflex to the food hitting his stomach. He had poor muscle tone and could never really run or play any other sports, though he was allowed to participate on the school's soccer team. His lifelong physical challenges were many.

He wrestled with the effects of his illness and was then consigned to a wheelchair. I remember my father and mother would help to lift him in and out of the car and my sister and I would push him through the hallways of our grade school. He underwent subsequent surgery to ease the immobility in his feet and legs and actually began walking with assistance the spring and summer of the year he died. Progress was being made; he had begun to do much better and had started to walk again. Paul seemed happy, and we were all hopeful. My mother spoke with enthusiasm on the day that he walked to meet our grandparents at the airport gate when they came to visit from Minnesota. However, tragically, a couple of weeks later, he experienced complications following a severe fever and he died from septic shock the next week in the emergency room. The young ER doctor on staff relayed this heartbreaking news to my anxiety-ridden parents in the waiting room. It was devastating.

Despite Paul's physical struggles, I will always remember his positive attitude, magnetic personality, enchanting and charming the nurses at the hospital, as well as our neighbors, his teachers, and schoolmates— all those he touched in his brief life. I know I am not alone in these memories of him and will hold dearly the golden moments we had together, of his cackly laugh and sparkly blue eyes.

Depression and detachment followed in my household. My father withdrew into studying to get his second master's degree; my mother suffered depression, escaped to her bedroom, watching TV, and reading books. I was left in a sad sorrowful place and had to continue the life of a fifteen-year-old teenager. Our family of five was now reduced to four. I remember setting the table in the days, weeks, and months that followed Paul's death, choking back tears as I realized there was an empty seat at the table that would never again be filled. We tried to continue living, but what was it for? Life was so fragile and unfair. In what world is it normal for a parent to bury a child? Where was the hope we needed to carry on?

My sister Katy has always been the self-possessed, resourceful, and self-assured child of our family. I, on the other hand, was the artist, maybe the one who thought a little too much and stayed in my head philosophizing and daydreaming; I was prone to melancholy at times too, especially after his death. Katy was the eldest child, two years older than me. She was athletic, the homecoming queen in college, and a real go-getter. Of course, she was very sad about losing our brother Paul, and grieved in her own way; we all did. I think she and I both saw my mother and father's outward grief and tried to hide ours just for the sake of picking up and getting back to living a normal life. And, as is typical of an eldest child, perhaps she took on some responsibility in keeping the family intact. After Paul's death, Katy maintained her rigorous athletic schedule, kept up good grades, and also had the idea of getting a puppy for the family, with whom we all fell in love, most especially my father. I owe a lot to her for keeping things in proper perspective, finding humor when necessary and, in short, for looking out for me throughout my entire life.

Yet how could I go back into high school and worry about and relate to what my friends were shallowly concerned about? Hair styles. Shopping. Their latest crush. I had just had a huge piece ripped out of my heart, my beloved younger brother, gone far too soon. I had experienced a tragedy, and I did not feel that life was worth living any more than my mother did. The pain was too great; a huge part of me was gone, never to return. What did come into focus for me at that time, however, was the brevity and fragility of life, the realization that we are here for only a short time. My overall perspective had changed and, as Langston Hughes so beautifully described, "My soul had grown deep like the rivers." Paul certainly had a powerful impact on my life. He is an angel now, and I know we will meet again.

About three years after my brother's passing, I was driving down to school one evening in North Carolina. The sky was dark but clear and the song "Tears in Heaven" by Eric Clapton came on the radio. It is about Eric's son who died tragically after falling out of a window. I was missing my brother and I said, "just give me a sign, Paul," and not a moment later I saw the longest shooting star I'd ever seen streak across the night sky right in front of me. I started crying, as I was quite moved by this. What a beautiful moment to keep and treasure! My heart felt at ease and at peace immediately and the experience made me even more of a believer than ever in synchronicities, the heavenly miracles in our midst. Those are the things we cannot see but can feel and understand as messages from angels on the other side of the veil of life.

Inspiration for Today:

Call upon the strength of a hero/heroine you have admired in the past. If, for example, it is Quan Yin, I would print out a card-size image of her, put it in front of you during a meditation, and ask for any wisdom or strength from her. I have also done this with Archangel Michael, Archangel Gabriel, Maya Angelou, Joan of Arc, etc. Calling forth a deity or spiritual figure can be a very powerful thing.

THE IMPORTANCE
OF GRATITUDE

*Wear gratitude like a cloak and it will
feed every corner of your life.*

– Rumi

When all is falling apart, find something, even just one thing, to be grateful for; this is absolutely the essential ingredient in healing your heart. When your mind is focused on all that is going wrong, see if you can find one thing that is going right.

Gratitude can be simple and yet it is such a profound, powerful practice. In truth, it is the basic tenet and fundamental requirement for manifesting a shift, a needed change, and a transformation in you and in your life.

I was adopted when I was just two weeks old.

My biological mother located me when I was thirty years old and pregnant with my first child. I had been a surprise, she later relayed to me, as many of us are. But perhaps I was meant to be here all along. And how does this shape a life? I suppose it helped me realize with an even greater degree of understanding that we are all autonomous human beings, that we are separate from any birth dossier, all on our own unique paths and individual journeys. However, I know I am not unique; many people have stories of foster care and adoption and other biological discoveries to tell, and mine is just another one. So, although I could look at my story as one of rejection, I have chosen to see how wanted and loved I actually was (because, in fact, I *am* so loved by my adopted family!). And it has reminded me that when we turn the prism, we can see a whole new world of possibility. Neither of my biological parents had any other children after I was born. I have met them, and I am enjoying getting to know them both, individually. I do share some very uncanny similarities and traits with each of them. I have inherited my artistic skills from my biological mother as we have a very distinct line to our drawings. My aunt on my paternal side is an artist as well, so I suppose it was inevitable that creative genes got passed along.

My interest in guitar and music most definitely came from my biological father, who sings and plays guitar. It was strange the day he and I both met: our conversation gravitated to our musical tastes, and we found similarities in the music we listen to and play. Neither one of us could believe it. We both owned Martin acoustic guitars. We both love and listen to '70s classical rock and classic country music songs, our favorites among the many, ranging from The Allman Brothers, Bob Dylan, Johnny Cash, Townes Van Zandt, and JJ Cale. It was a very strange coincidence indeed, and one which may speak to our DNA and ancestral history!

Another strange synchronicity is the fact that my biological father also shares the same name and birthday as my younger brother, Paul, who passed. That is just too much of a coincidence to deny. A girlfriend who has met both my adopted parents and my biological parents said to me, "you are a wonderful combination of them all, and you are unique unto yourself also." In the end, I believe I am here because I am supposed to be here, and I was given to the family that God and the Universe intended me to be raised by. For that, I am enormously grateful as my adopted parents were two wonderful, tremendous people who became my parents in every sense of the word: they were kind, loving, supportive, honest, and morally and ethically driven. There is just no other way my story was to be written.

And so I ask, today, are you able to look across the room at someone you love? Can you go outside and take a breath of fresh air? Did your feet hit the floor next to your bed this morning? Are you walking and talking? Are you able to take a hot shower? Do you have heat when it's cold outside? Can you smile? Do you have a good sense of humor? A good friend? Can you say a prayer of gratitude for at least one of these? I recently found this journal entry, written when my marriage was falling apart and the wheels were falling right off the cart. I knew somewhere I just had to cling to something and here is where it started and what I wrote. Instead of counting the things I was losing, I began counting the things that I was lucky to have:

Help me to appreciate the beauty even in the sad and grieving moments.

I have fulfilling, enriching, ever-expanding friendships and relationships.

I trust there is an order to things.

I have so much to be thankful for: my health, my talents, my desires.

I have all the strength I need inside of me. I just need to summon it from the Universe.

I have access to all the power and can become empowered by the wonderfully vast and limitless Source.

I have many gifts to share.
I will rise up like the phoenix.
I have wisdom. I am blessed.
I trust the Universe knows what it is doing.

Inspiration for Today:

Think of one thing you are grateful for every morning. Then try for three, expanding your list regularly. You can recite this list quietly to yourself, write the things for which you are grateful in a journal, or even list them on your calendar. If you do this every day, your life will change.

THE IMPORTANCE
OF MINGLING
WITH NATURE

In every walk with nature,
one receives far more than he seeks.

– John Muir

Nature can be an inexpensive, accessible, quick, and easy remedy, a natural and organic panacea for the spirit and soul. It whispers its sweet songs in a kind of lullaby, with its very own score of rhythms, harmonies, and tempo. There is brilliant design in it, if we will just bear it witness and carve out the time to enjoy it, no matter how briefly—even if only during a small lunch break. It will enrich your experience all the more if you take your shoes off and feel the dirt, grass, rocks, sand, or cool water beneath your feet. The earth can ease your burdens and com-post your problems if you put your feet in it, so let it. If you live in the city, go find a park. If you are near the ocean or a mountain, you know where to go!

Tune in to each one of your senses. Listen to the sounds, the ones close by and the ones far away. Notice and name all the various colors and hues around you, notice the light and shadows, the shapes, and textures all around you. Close your eyes and ears and concen-trate on what you smell. Notice the taste in your mouth. Feel the air on your skin and the ground beneath you. Touch the grass, a tree, a rock, or some earth with your fingers, too. Open all your senses now and let yourself enjoy them all. You will gain much from any amount of time spent outside, I assure you.

The Lenard Effect—also called "spray electrifica-tion" and the "waterfall effect"—describes the height-ened production of negative ions near waterfalls, rivers, and oceans. These negative ions—essentially specially-charged molecules floating in the air or atmosphere—are said to help elevate mood levels. I happen to believe there is a positive effect to be sure.

Inspiration for Today:

Go on a hike or walk around the block, look up, look down. Leave your digital devices at home, even headphones or earbuds with music or meditations. Just let your senses come alive.

THE IMPORTANCE OF CREATING CEREMONY: HONORING BEGINNINGS & ENDINGS

All the darkness of the world cannot
extinguish the light of a single candle.

– St. Francis of Assisi

Ceremony, or ritual, can be very cathartic. It can assist when you are in transition, be it professional or personal, when you are experiencing anxiety or conflict, or simply at a crossroads in your life. Ceremony can be used to honor beginnings and endings, to let go of the old and bring in the new, and to do so faster. It can also be used to offer gratitude and appreciation to the Universe.

Folklore asserts that when a soul passes, a bird enters the room. I have a very vivid memory of when I was sitting bedside while my father took his last breaths during the final stages of battling pancreatic cancer. I heard a bird flapping its wings so loudly, I looked under the bed and pulled the curtains back. No bird inside. I didn't see any bird outside, either, flapping at the window to come in, as much as it sounded like that's what was happening. It remains a mystery to behold, but one that remains intensely profound and quite sacred to me. It begs the question, at what point does a soul separate and leave its body? And how does it ascend?

While a funeral may be one form of ceremony most mature adults will have experienced in their lives, there are other ways to mark transitions and ease our pain. A ceremony does not have to be elaborate and complicated and does not have to be a public event. In fact, sometimes, the simpler the message you send out, the better.

Here are three simple but quite meaningful and powerful ceremonies you might consider incorporating into your daily life:

Pitch It

I call this Pitching It to the Universe. It helps, at the crossroads and transitions of your life, with celebrating joys and releasing sorrows.

Start by writing down a few things you wish to add to or subtract from your life. Find a small stone or rock that fits nicely in the palm of your hand. Take a few moments to find your quiet still point and ask Source to be with you. Then, take a deep breath, and pause. With your eyes closed, exhale deeply, elongating the exhale, and, concentrating on your lower abdomen, breathe in and up through your lungs, and then blow into the rock, invoking your intentions. Turn the rock three times, blowing into three of its sides. Then, making sure there is no one in your path, pitch it! You have done all you can do. Sit in stillness for another moment, and smile: you have officially turned it over to the Universe.

Bury It

You can also write your intentions on a strip of paper (compostable is always best), wrap the paper around a rock, and follow a similar breathing pattern as described above, blowing your intentions into the rock or paper. Bury the rock and paper, again handing everything over to the earth.

For instance, if you are getting ready to sell your house, state your gratitude on the piece of paper and tell the house how much it has meant to you. Bless it and give it thanks. Bury the note on the property as a way to close and clean up the entangled ties that can often accompany the emotions of leaving a house we once inhabited for months, if not years. It is wise to honor the things that have been good to us, in this case, that which has given us shelter. I like to give thanks to the house, bless it, and say, "We've had a good run, and now change is necessary for my growth and well-being." I have held these types of prayer circles and ceremonies with my children on the cusp of a move into a new house or to a new state.

Burn It

In my studies with Alberto Villoldo, I learned that a fire ceremony can be a perfect and beautiful way to release our old stories. Fire makes for a powerful, sacred ceremony and is probably the oldest ancestral tradition found in many cultures worldwide. You can make a bonfire or light an outdoor fire pit, make a tiny fire in a metal bowl, or even simply light a candle. Write your intentions on a slip of paper. Remember, we are writing down the things we wish to bring in or let go (either sending an intention to welcome in something new or let something go that no longer serves you). Blow your intentions or wishes into the piece of paper, or, if you are using a small stick, blow into the stick. Next place it into the fire, you have done all you can do, now you are giving it over to the Universe. Allow the energy that was wrapped around that story to be released and transmute it back into light. Pass your hands over the fire, where the smoke is being released, and bring your hands to your abdomen, your heart, and your forehead (the mind's eye).

These were lessons the Universe was offering you. In your mind or aloud, declare, "I now release this/you to the Universe." A fire ceremony will help you repair and regenerate, and shed the old stories or beliefs that you hold about people or things in your life. You can say, "I release you to your destiny." You can even go further and say, "I release you to your destiny and I release you with love." It is the intention that is most important here, and this helps to find what I call right relation with the things and people in your life. In essence, you are tidying up the energetic connections that so often entangle or enmesh us and which become unhealthy or toxic. Sometimes the right relation I am speaking of is with ourselves—the most important relationship of all and the one most worthy of our investment of time and energy.

Inspiration for Today:

Find your own place near a body of water, river, stream, pond, lake, or ocean. Find a stone. Sit in this stillness. Listen to the sounds of the wind, water, birds, animals. Say a prayer. Release it and let go.

CONNECTING TO SOURCE OR DIVINE GUIDANCE

*Although you appear in earthly form your
essence is pure Consciousness. You are the
fearless guardian of Divine Light. So come,
return to the root of the root of your own soul.*

– Rumi

When I talk about Source, or the Universe, or God, please know that I'm talking about a much broader entity than the religion/religious factions that man has created. I am referring to infinite intelligence, divine guidance and wisdom, life force itself, consciousness, the eternalness-of-all-that-we-are, our soul energy, that which connects us to our very essence, our spiritual selves, and our eternal selves. This life force, which is present in all sentient beings, connects us and flows through us, acting as an internal light of love and energy in all that we are, possess, and radiate. Sometimes, we need to remember this, to surrender to this higher power, to put aside our need to try to control things beyond the scope of that which we can control, to give up the reins and trust that there is a current running underneath and throughout for our greater good.

Intuition

One of my college friends—an old roommate—suffered for many long years with Multiple Sclerosis (MS). Sommer had been diagnosed soon after she was married. She and her husband decided to have a baby knowing that perhaps the disease could worsen, as sometimes will happen after a pregnancy. Her MS in fact, did progress after her daughter, Abby, was born, and she became quite debilitated. In subsequent years, Sommer lost the use of her legs and arms. She could no longer bathe or shower without help. Confined to a bed and able to use only a wheelchair, she managed to live some semblance of a life, and, with the tremendous help of and support of her family, a daytime nurse, and her ex-husband, she raised her daughter. My friend, Molly, and I would visit, taking Sommer out on day trips to the pool, to run errands or get coffee, and even to a live concert now and then, rolling her wheelchair in the back of her handicapped wheelchair-accessible van and onto the musical venue of choice.

Molly and I tried to visit her often. We would make her meals, play music, sing and dance. Once we painted her room turquoise. We did her hair, nails and makeup, and one visit I even took some sexy boudoir shots of her in pretty lingerie. We had fun together—anything to help Sommer feel she was loved and cherished and to help her know that although situations may change, our friendship was steadfast.

On one occasion, we managed to take her to the beach. Although it was not far from her house, she hadn't been in years. With the help of a lifeguard, we moved her into a beach chair that was able to roll over the sand. When Molly and I got Sommer down to the water, she broke into tears at the sight of it. Molly and I poured the ocean water over her feet as she inhaled the salt air. It was Sommer's 50th birthday, and it was a good day. In the years that followed, it seemed she would steadily lose ground with every passing month: she needed tremendous help with every aspect of her life, and eventually lost the ability to speak and feed herself, too.

A year before Sommer passed, I painted a large picture of Bahamian clouds and skies hoping somehow this would transport her to a place where we could not physically take her. Last January I dreamed she visited me. She told me very matter-of-factly that she was going to die in September. I was surprised, of course, to hear this very specific time frame, though somehow comforted by the fact that Sommer was not emotional—not crying—when she said it. Molly and I had planned to visit her in October that year, on her birthday. Of course, when the month of September came, I was a little on edge.

Sommer's brother texted me on the morning of Friday, September 23, and said that she was not doing well. I jumped in my car and went to visit her. She recognized me and could nod her head and whisper a few words, and we could make out some sentences. She told the live-in nurse that she wanted me to spend the night, so I did, but I slept with one eye open as I listened to her oxygen machine. The next day, Sommer rallied a little. Her daughter Abby, now quite grown up, was coming to visit and she was excited to see her. I played her favorite music and danced to Jerry Garcia and Pink Floyd, and we enjoyed our time together. That same day, Sommer told me she loved me and that I was a good friend. But when Sunday came, she closed her eyes, never to open them again. She died five days later. I still miss her terribly, but no one should have to live a life imprisoned in a body like that. I am at peace knowing she flies free with angels now.

Other Synchronicities

I've had many other instances of the synchronicities and the undeniable energetic ties that connect us. For example, I was chaperoning for my daughter's volleyball tournament in Virginia one weekend and was watching the match on Saturday when I got a real intuitive feeling that I needed to step away from the game and text my son, as there was weather approaching the East Coast. It was a wintry mix, as we call it around Washington, D.C. When I texted him and asked him how the weather was, he said, "I just hit a tree in the car. The airbags went off, but we are okay. Will's father is coming to get us."

Another incident occurred when I was hiking with a friend on a tough trail one August in Great Falls, Maryland. It is known as the Billy Goat trail as it is very difficult—full of rocks and drop offs into the Potomac River, and sharp precipices. My friend and I had worn the right clothes for the hot day but chose to go at noon when the sun was at its most intense. We didn't bring any water with us as we were planning on a milder hike. Somehow, we got sidetracked and wound up on the highest peaks and most difficult trails in the park. No one was on our trail, as it was a much too hot and humid day. We felt stuck in a hard place. Should we continue to hike, or should we turn back? I had two large lemonades for us in the car but that didn't do us much good at all. I began to feel lightheaded in the heat but tried to keep a positive attitude. We lost sight of the markers for the trail. We stopped to rest and realized our clothes were soaked through. I had begun to grow more concerned when a young twenty-something with a backpack came upon us out of nowhere. We asked him if he knew where the trail was and if we could follow him. It was very rocky, and really there was no trail at all; we were just rock climbing at this point. Miraculously, he had an extra water bottle in his bag and graciously gave us the bottle to share. He was an angel, and very patient as he led us back down to safety. He waited for us at every turn, looking over his shoulder. I asked him what his name was, and he said "Jake." I had learned earlier that year that my cousin had a friend whose son died in the mountains in an accident. He had been a wilderness Emergency Medical Technician (EMT), and his name was Jake. Coincidence? I think not! It is quite clear to me that there are angels here working for and among us. *Thank you, Jake. You saved us that day.*

I believe that regardless of our chosen or preferred religion, divine guidance exists for us all. We are being guided by unseen forces: some of us, at times, may experience signs, messages, or occurrences of grace, bearing witness to their inexplicable presence, both big and small. Perhaps some of us tune in by way of our intuitive selves, feeling a gentle nudge to "go this way." Or we may experience subtle daily coincidences or serendipitous events. You, yourself, may very well have witnessed a full-blown, real-life miracle, full of mystery and awe, that you or others simply could not explain. Do not discount any of these occurrences! It is all happening *for* you. Feel comfort in knowing you are not walking this life alone. You have a whole angelic army behind you. We often hear about our gut or our intuitive sense, but I think this also includes our heart. As we work and operate by intuition rather than just intelligence or intellect, and without judgment or ego, we experience exponential benefits. From this purity and clarity, we dwell in both a place of possibility and deeper knowing, with greater assurance and calm.

Inspiration for Today:

Look back at your day when it is done. What, if anything, was a touch on the side of the miraculous? Were there any messages that needed to come through? Did the post office employee or grocery store cashier tell you something that made you stop, pause, and smile? These were gifts to you and for you; learn from them and appreciate these messages even if they may seem, at the time, small and minute.

ON FEAR

Worry can give a small thing a big shadow.

– Swedish Proverb

Fear is one of the strongest emotions we experience. It can help us deal with a potentially perilous situation by giving us an adrenaline boost, but it's not so good when we are receiving a daily low-grade dose of it, which eventually wreaks havoc on our nervous system and our body. Fear and worry reveal to us that we are disconnected, and not allowing the essential healing flow of the Universe to come to us and through us. It has also been said that the word fear is an acronym that stands for "False Evidence Appearing Real."

When our minds are consumed by or clouded with fear, we find ourselves in a paralyzed state where we are often our own worst enemy. The first thing I do when I sense I am sliding into a fearful state is to ask myself, "What am I really afraid of?" What are the origins of this fear? Am I creating a "what-if" situation? Has it happened yet? What is the worst-case scenario that I am creating? Is it factual or the product of my imagination? Under the scrutiny of these and other questions, the situation often sounds ridiculous because it is not substantiated at all. It loses its power and shrinks or vanishes altogether.

The night I asked for a divorce I had a vivid dream and woke up crying. My children were safe with their grandparents, and I was staying this first night with my cousins. But in the dream, I was in an airplane that crashed into the water of an ocean. I remember thinking of swimming towards the light, up and out to the surface. My hands were in a prayer position. I was fearing for my children—where were they? When I came to the surface, I saw all three of them, safe in a lifeboat, buzzing over to me on the surface, safe in the vessel. There was a lot of sunlight. Immediately I knew *and felt* we were all going to be okay.

When the fight, flight, or freeze reaction* kicks in, fueled by the false tales we create, it can do real damage, wreaking havoc on our bodies and our healthy cells and immune systems.

In turn, our chakras are connected to our nervous systems, as well as to our respiratory, circulatory, digestive, excretory, and cardiovascular systems. So, it's little wonder that when we experience a fear-tension-pain cycle, our bodies are negatively affected: in essence we block healthy, normal, flow and function.

Let's take a deeper look at the chakras, since they are so vitally important to our health and wellbeing. The chakras are energy centers in your body through which energy flows. There are seven major chakras on the physical body:

- crown chakra
- third eye chakra
- throat chakra
- heart solar chakra
- solar plexus chakra
- sacral chakra
- root chakra

Now, imagine them opening and closing at varying times of the day—truly a dynamic system indeed. If these centers are blocked, or stuck, illness can result.

---

* also known as the fear-tension-pain syndrome

However, if we keep these energy centers flowing and free of any blockages, the result is a boost to our immunity. In turn, the more freely energy flows, the healthier we are.

It is possible to heal on a cellular level, and deeper study into energy fields, chakras, and epigenetics in recent years is now explaining how it all works. But not to worry—just as you do not have to know exactly how electricity works to power your home, so you do not need to know how our cells regenerate and heal, nor do you fully need to understand the study of metaphysical and quantum physics and how it so closely relates to us.

Inspiration for Today:

Look back over your day and ask yourself, what did I *not* do or act on because fear was impeding me? What did I make up about why I shouldn't do it? Where was the place of fear originating? This is a good practice for identifying any false narratives we create.

EMBRACING
UNCERTAINTY

*What we know is little, what we
don't know is immense.*

—Pierre-Simon Laplace

To move forward into wholeness, we have to learn to be okay with uncertainty and turn our troubles over to a higher power; essentially, we need to give up control. A lot of our fear resides in our desire for control.

In September of 2019, a Category 5 hurricane ripped through the small Bahamian island where we have a family home and where I had formerly owned and operated an art gallery. My first concern was for my friends in the tight-knit community with whom I had lost contact with overnight. Word got out the next day that many lives were indeed spared (miraculously!)

on the island, but on the neighboring island, tragically, many lives were lost. It was a horrible series of events to witness; the mass destruction and sheer devastation, but more than that, the tremendous toll that it had taken on the community—on both an individual level and collectively—was immense. The weather programs and news channels back in the states were showing horrific pictures of the mass wreckage; it was incomprehensible, like nothing I had ever witnessed before. The island was unrecognizable. The trees had been sheared off, and not one green leaf was left on anything. It looked like a war-torn country where a bomb had just gone off. One needed to wear lace up boots to walk around all the debris and rubble; it would be a long time before open toed shoes were worn in this island town again. Our world had been flooded with loss and uncertainty. So many in the community had and still have their own unique and harrowing stories. Many still live with the PTSD and the trauma caused by it. Four years later, I bear witness to so many of their painful memories which they need to recount to release and heal that which has been so painfully trapped within their bodies and minds.

The Effort to Rebuild

The hurricane had destroyed the airport and the docks on the island, so it took me two weeks to even coordinate a visit to look at the damage on a shared seaplane.

During that time, it rained constantly, which meant it rained inside my house, as I had no tarps yet, and the hurricane had punched holes in my roof. When I arrived on the scene, I was hit by the smell I won't soon forget of mold and rot from surrounding collapsing structures. Inside my home, my refrigerator looked like a crime scene, and I'm still not sure what liquids were seeping out of it; so toxic that my builder's advice was just to get rid of it. And so I began the daunting task of rebuilding. In my heart it was worth the herculean effort because deep down some things are just worth fighting for, especially a true labor of love, which it was. Power was not restored for a whole year. During the first few months, I slept on my porch in a tent as my house was a total mess. I brought in hired help and friends, and made many trips to Home Depot, carrying in food and water from Florida on a chartered plane as I didn't want to tax the island's resources and its residents who were in greater need. My house needed to be emptied completely and so much furniture had to be thrown out. The mold throughout the house had to be expunged and eradicated. I could sometimes hear the tree rats (aka "Bahamian squirrels") at night getting into the food bags and a cooler I stashed next to my tent outside. We had no idea when our world would return to something we might call normal. But organizations like Samaritan's Purse were wonderful in helping residents rebuild, offering outside resources and support to restore the spirit of the community. The local Hope Town Volunteer Fire and Rescue members were an amazing asset to the community, and continue to be to this day. Food kitchens were organized and assembled in town. My former art gallery survived and was being used as the emergency stand-in health clinic. But by far the most memorable and heroic acts were those disguised within the community—those people who offered to help their neighbor even when their own lives and homes were torn apart. Despite all of this and the total loss, most likely totaling billions of dollars, I witnessed locals, really good people with big hearts, doing kind things. In fact, this is the greatest example of God working through us and among us.

I can honestly say it was worth the effort to rebuild in the end. My children and I have had so many happy memories there. Plus, I started my art gallery business there, my first foray into a career post-divorce, and it was something of which I was incredibly proud. Indeed it was difficult losing something I had worked so hard for, but I'll never forget those who helped me in the aftermath. I am deeply grateful.

I have been on a journey of finding a healing path yielding gifts of wisdom, clarity, and peace. I know I cannot predict the future, nor do I have control over any of it, just as I do not have control over the actions of others. I know and have to believe that there will be good things in store for me, no matter how difficult the endeavor. I often tell the Universe, "I remain open to your suggestions. I am willing to live with uncertainty.

I am open to witness the mystery and grow in these challenges given to me." For I *know* that the Universe can create a much better story than I could ever imagine on my own. This is truly dwelling in possibility, living with both the uncertainties but also remaining open to life's magical moments.

Inspiration for Today:

If the goal is to live or dwell in possibility, I sometimes ask my Reiki clients to turn their "What Is" statements into "What Ifs." For example, I am driving a decent car which I like and had some happy memories in, although it's an older model, and it doesn't quite have the up-to-date electronics that I'd like to have. It has a lot of miles and is needing more and more attention and repairs (*What Is*). However, *What If* next year I received the bonus I was hoping for with work, and I could finally put the money down on a new car that I've had my eye on, and then, I'll take that vision a bit further. I am driving on a weekend road trip with my best friend to a music festival—the windows are down, and we are having uplifting and inspiring conversations as we go. There is a new car smell, a great soundtrack on, a full tank of gas, we've experienced no traffic, and there's a cooler packed full of snacks and drinks. Now, you write down examples of this for yourself. You may find your What If scenarios becoming quite creative, detailed, and fun.

THE IMPORTANCE OF REDUCING THE STEADY STREAM OF TOXINS IN THE NEWS & ON SOCIAL MEDIA

All men's miseries derive from not being
able to sit in a quiet room alone.

— Blaise Pascal

Human beings simply aren't meant to take the world's entire store of information into our brains and clamp all its tragedies and problems onto our shoulders, which is why I believe the 24/7 cycle of radio, TV, newspapers, and social media delivers too much for any one person to process.

Yet, when most of us are in pain, the times when we need solitude the most, we turn to the internet, our phones and mobile devices, and the television for distraction or solace. But we simply must clear out this toxicity if we want to facilitate healing.

News incites fear and as I tell my children, "You will never experience a spiritual awakening when you are on your phones." Electronic devices should be at our service, and not the other way around. They are not our masters. Put them down, look up, look out, look inward. It's a beautiful world, you don't want to miss it.

I suggest taking frequent news and phone fasts, also known as "news sobriety." Make one day a week (or at least an entire day of every month) phone-free or media-free, and I bet this will come to be your favorite day.

What can you do in the time you are not on your phone or scrolling the internet? The practices in this book! Discover the act of loving solitude, which is quite a different experience from the feeling of loneliness. Go for a walk, go for a hike. Take yourself on a date, out to dinner or to a theater production or live music concert.

When I eat out, I like to bring along a book to read; this tells others I am completely content to dine alone (and I am!). If you do this regularly, one day you will reach the state of being in blissful solitude, which is quite different from being alone or lonely. This might not come right away; it is almost a practice—a habit— but it's wonderful to learn to love spending time alone with yourself. This is a state within you that simply must be reached if you are to heal completely. Enjoy the simple pleasures life has to offer and enjoy *you*.

Inspiration for Today:

Notice how good you feel when you disconnect from outside interference and connect with yourself. Carve out the time, perhaps on a Sunday afternoon, to pack a picnic, go to a museum, leave it all behind, enjoy your self-care time. It can be quite fun and empowering.

THE IMPORTANCE OF TAKING CARE OF YOUR BODY: GET YOUR SLEEP, EAT HEALTHY FOODS & MOVE

For each new morning with its light,
for rest and shelter of the night.
For health and food for love and friends,
for everything thy goodness sends.

—Ralph Waldo Emerson

Security, food, and shelter—these needs must be established first and foremost, as they are fundamental to your core being. Beyond your basic needs, try to focus on improving your sleep, your diet, your hydration, and try to move every day.

Sleep

Good rest is essential for enhancing creativity and critical problem solving, and for overall brain and cognitive skill functioning. An article from *Medical News Today*[**] cites these benefits:

1) Better memory and performance
2) Lower weight gain risk
3) Better calorie regulation
4) Greater athletic performance
5) Lower risk of heart disease
6) More emotional and social intelligence
7) Prevention of depression
8) Lower inflammation
9) A stronger immune system

To maximize your opportunities for a great sleep, make sure you sleep in a place that is as dark as possible and keep your room temperature cool. Turning off screens is of utmost importance. Use an old-fashioned

---

[**]Jenna Fletcher, Why Sleep is Essential for Health States," Medical News Today, January 6, 2023, https://www.medical-newstoday.com/articles/325353

alarm clock or, if you must use your phone alarm, place it across the room from you with its airplane mode activated. I also suggest you keep TVs, magazines, newspapers, and food out of your sleeping space. Keep your space tidy. Do not store anything under your bed. Make your bed every day and ensure there is good air circulation around your sleeping space. If possible, try to go to bed at around the same time every evening. Morning and evening minutes should be sacred. Gently begin your day and gently end it. Bookending, I call it. A book of poetry, a cup of tea, a lit candle, a quiet evening walk are all perfect ways to bookend your days.

Healthy Eating

Fresh food is medicine, full of life force and healing energy. Buy vegetables at your local farmer's market. Start a small garden, even if it includes only tomatoes and herbs in a planter or on your deck. Fresh food carries energy from the sun. Be sure to get enough good fats and protein in your diet from nuts, seeds, avocados, and fish, if you eat it, to ensure that your brain has what it needs to function properly. Eat plenty of fiber from vegetables and eat your meal slowly with awareness, and with no electronic devices to disturb your meal. Fresh food not only looks good with its intense, varied colors, but it also tastes delicious. Have a family meal at least once a week. Light a candle and make it special. Of course, say grace and a blessing together before you indulge. This is an old practice our ancestors created that many of us have somehow, sadly, gotten away from. Perhaps the blessing will even have a positive effect on your food.

Water

Most people are chronically dehydrated, which can cause irritability, anxiety, fatigue, headaches, and a false sense of hunger. Drink a tall glass of water when you first wake up and again before or with each meal. Drink non-caffeinated herbal tea and eat hydrating fresh fruits. It is not just water that our bodies need, but electrolytes. Electrolytes help keep the body balanced, replenish low reserves, and combat fatigue. Some ways of consuming these necessary minerals to achieve optimal health would be adding electrolyte tablets or powders to your drink, drinking coconut water (my favorite), or even a pinch of salt! Well-hydrated people feel better and feeling better *physically* helps you feel better *mentally*. Adding a few drops of lemon juice to your water quenches your thirst and adds vitamin C, too. I'm also a big fan of steeping freshly grated ginger, honey, and lemon in hot water when I'm starting to feel a little under the weather. My kids come home and request it often! There is something quite healing and soothing to the soul in a hot cup of tea.

Movement

At the very least, wake up your spinal column with some morning stretches. Stretching invigorates your spine and your central nervous system—it helps to think of your spine and brain as what they truly are: a command center for your whole body. So, when you wake up your spine first, it helps turn all the lights on. We also need daily stretches to keep our body feeling well, nimble, and in a good place. This is especially true if you sit or travel a lot. A wise man once told me, "motion is lotion." We should strive for some sort of physical exercise every day. Long walks are the secret to longevity. And remember, exercise is just as important for our mental health as it is for our physical health.

Inspiration for Today:

Find a local farmers market and buy some produce to make a fresh meal. You can also cut, peel, and prepare veggies, fruits, and other snacks/meals in advance for your week to come. Then, just grab and go!

THE IMPORTANCE OF FINDING A STILL POINT & MEDITATING AT LEAST ONCE DAILY

Real action is in the silent moments.

—Ralph Waldo Emerson

T he idea that there is a relationship between fear, our mind, and pain is not new. Aristotle wrote of the mind-body connection in his teachings and emphasized the importance of deep relaxation, especially during birth, around 300 B.C.

I am not suggesting that this is for everyone but, as I mentioned earlier, the hypnobirthing training I undertook in preparation for my children's arrivals did show me a map of how to get to the still point within me. Hippocrates wrote about childbirth and midwifery, and Aristotle emphasized the importance of deep relaxation. A natural childbirth promotes the belief that we must surrender to the process, that our bodies know what to do, and that there is a flow and rhythm available to us, a greater wisdom, if we just release ourselves to it. Rather than trying to control birth, we can surrender to it, free of fear. I maintain that in deep relaxation we are fully present and fully aware of our surroundings, instead of what might be perceived as "sleeping" or "being out of it" or in a kind of deep hypnosis.

We are tuned in on many levels of consciousness. That is what we strive for in our place of meditation or deep relaxation...and one can apply it to so much in life. Finding your still point, or the calmest place in your mind, takes a little practice. But the good thing is that if you find it once, it will seem like you've created an internal map, and it becomes increasingly easy to get to it, much like coming home to the house where you live.

Centering

Your still time can include meditation, sometimes referred to as centering. To meditate, just be still for anywhere from five to thirty minutes. You can sit in a chair or on the floor or lie down on a pile of pillows. Just do so without interruption and try to do it at the same time of day for the same length of time on a consistent basis.

We take 20,000 breaths of precious oxygen a day. Thoughts will come through your mind and interrupt your focus on your breath. Notice the thoughts, watch them come and watch them go, and return to focus on your breathing. Try it with a smile on your face. Let go and know you cannot get this wrong. Appreciate the delicious and abundant, ever-essential, always-available oxygen!

There are many different breathing techniques that are beneficial and here are a couple I love:

Find a comfortable position, seated or lying prone. Inhale to the count of three, find space at the top of the breath and pause for a moment. Then, exhale to the count of five, almost as if you were descending on a roller coaster. The more comfortable you become, the more you will be able to extend the out breath even more, maybe even stretching it to seven seconds. After a few minutes, return to regular breath. This simple technique is easy and can help us to regain groundedness, to reset our nervous system and move us from a sympathetic to parasympathetic state, achieving a more regulated, deeper state of relaxation where we are primed for messages and healing; connected and communing with our higher selves.

Then there is the Ujjayi breath, also called the "ocean breath." Soften the back of your throat on the exhale and hear the ocean in your breath. Feel the in-out rhythm of the as your breath flows in and out, like the ocean waves and tide. Keep repeating. I also enjoy lighting a candle and, with eyes open gently, focusing on it. The flame will jump and move, but that can serve as a reminder of our own thoughts, rising and falling, dancing, and changing shape, but never moving too far from the origin, always returning to the center of the wick.

Facial relaxation is also important. When the muscles in your face are relaxed, your body can follow. Try this now, if you can: lie down and gently close your eyelids and relax your forehead. Let your lips fall slightly apart. Your jaw will follow. Visualize your shoulders opening out and your head and body making a dent in the pillow or mattress underneath you. Arms and legs should feel heavy and limp. I like to place both hands on my heart or one hand on my heart and one on my abdomen.

The Power of Visualizations and Intentions (aka the Power of Prayer)

You can also use your still point time to set an intention. Close your eyes, exhale, and allow yourself to visualize and fantasize. Visualization simply refers to powerfully focused thoughts represented in the pictures of the mind's eye, and it causes equally powerful feelings. Think about your short-term and long-term goals. Before you wrap up, make sure you set your expectations for the immediate day ahead. Focus on what you wish for and see it fall effortlessly, easily, smoothly, and in perfect timing, into place. Carving out these precious minutes can mean resetting the course of your day. Sometimes I send out a request that my guides and angels prepare the way and space before I get to where I need to be for the day. This process has not disappointed me yet! So go ahead and try it—ask your guides to help prepare the space and day ahead.

Inspiration for Today:

I recommend finding a drumming circle in your area or sign up for a sound bath healing session. I am seeing more and more of this type of classes offered these days, and I think you will recognize the benefits immediately. These kinds of sessions can cleanse negative energy and emotions, assist in deep relaxation, and increase energy flow, creativity, and motivation.

THE IMPORTANCE
OF AFFIRMATIONS
& JOURNALING

*Lift up the Self by the Self and don't let the
Self droop down. For the Self is the Self's only
friend and the Self is the Self's only foe.*

—Bhagavad Gita

More self-love, less self-doubt. We all doubt and second guess ourselves at times—let's try harder to drop this bad habit! Remember to practice self-care, not self-sabotage. Stop the mind when it starts in on the criticisms, worries, and fears. After all, your thoughts are powerful, and your body, mind, and spirit are absolutely affected by them. As humans, we have the power to direct our thoughts where we want them to go, but that's something we often forget. We get hijacked by repetitive thoughts and beliefs that do not serve and support us.

Imagine if you were consistently focused on positive messages instead of negative self-talk. This is where affirmations—positive, uplifting statements—come into play. They are tools for the mind that are meant to be repeated and they can help brighten your outlook and improve your mindset. Using affirmations is like changing the dial on the radio—you switch from a station that is not serving you well to one that will help you reach your highest potential. Slowly your thoughts, beliefs, and life will upgrade to meet your affirmation.

When I am on the treadmill at the gym, in the shower, on a walk, or in the car, I like to repeat the words, "Healthy mind, healthy body, healthy spirit."

When I was going through a difficult time, my affirmation was a prayer:

> Dear God, please help me through this time of my life. I will now allow all good things to flow swiftly and easily into my life. For I am grateful for all my earthly blessings.

I invite you to create your own prayer.

The Power of Affirmations

The first step in benefitting from the power of affirmations lies in becoming aware of your negative self-talk and thoughts, also known as your "monkey mind."

Choose an affirmation that flips or transforms your negative thinking pattern by reinforcing something positive.

Here are some examples of affirmations:

I am safe.
I am okay.
I will get through this.
I am free.
I am alive.
I have value.
I have purpose.
I have worth.
I am loved.
I can love.
I am powerful.
I am creating rituals that support my well-being.
I am grounded.
I have free will.
I can only make decisions about me and my life.
I am the creator of my own reality.
My challenges are here as opportunities for growth and expansion.
I am ready for what comes next.
I invite peace.
I invite harmony.
I am focused on abundance.

It has been suggested that another way to do these affirmations is to hold your hands over a chakra while you are seated or lying prone and repeat affirmations that are aligned with that chakra's area of influence. You would start with your root chakra and repeat the practice as you work upwards towards your seventh chakra, then end with your hands over your third eye chakra. (Please refer to the list of chakras on page 45 in the "On Fear" chapter.)

For example, you would begin focusing on the root chakra with a basic "I am..." affirmation and then move upward to the sacral chakra, and say, "I feel..." The next affirmation would be at the solar plexus chakra where you would say, "I have..." and then you would move to the heart chakra where you would say, "I love..." The next stop would be the throat chakra where you would say "I speak..." and then you would move up to the third-eye chakra where you would say, "I see..." and finally we would end at the crown chakra, where we would say, "I know..."

Repeat the affirmations out loud and in your head. Some people write them on paper and stick them on the mirror or refrigerator. I once made a laminated piece of paper that I carried around in my wallet for years:

I am a strong, intelligent, wise woman.

I am a loving and nurturing mother.

I am loved and supported by my family.

I have loving and steadfast friendships.

I have all the tools I need to navigate through rough waters and to find the best, clear, and direct course.

My talents will be utilized and will realize their full potential.

Those things that challenge us, empower us.

Blessings will be abundant for me and my children in this life.

I will be happy!

Years later when I was in another period of crisis, I found in the bottom of a moving box the same laminated page with these affirmations again, and next to it, was my son's Lego sword no less, a clear and profound message from the Universe.

Inspiration for Today:

Create your own affirmations or prayers to turn to when you need support. I like keeping a notepad of paper on my bedside table and jotting them down at night or in the morning. Carry them with you on a piece of laminated paper in your wallet.

THE IMPORTANCE OF BREAKING FREE FROM THE VICTIM ROLE & REWRITING YOUR STORY

If there is no struggle, there is no progress.

—Frederick Douglass

Our spirits want to soar, and joy is our birthright! But we will never have a chance at transformation if we continue to tell the same stories and stay stuck in our victim roles. It's possible to break free, stop telling our tragic stories, and release our victim roles.

In fact, if we don't address these obstacles in our lives, whatever they may be—a toxic relationship, a sadness, a grief, or some other source of suffering—disease and sickness will manifest in our bodies.

We'll never ascend out of the negative state in which we find ourselves if we hold ourselves hostage to those old stories. After all, no one gets out of here without challenges, and they can either bring us down and take us out, or we can use them to become better versions of ourselves.

Starting at around the age of eighteen and all the way through my thirties, my romantic relationships all seemed to carry a common denominator: all were with men who were highly volatile—they seemed to possess explosive tempers, harbor a jealous, controlling, and possessive side, were adept at gaslighting, and embraced duplicitous patterns and traits reminiscent of Dr. Jekyll and Mr. Hyde. Why I put up with it or allowed it for so many years, I cannot say. I can only surmise that I stayed with these men for so long because I wasn't a quitter. I didn't walk away when things got hard, even though I didn't deserve that kind of treatment. When I did decide to walk away, at least I could say I did my part, and I did the best I could.

When I think back to my childhood, my first teachers were my parents who had a loving and steadfast relationship, and I therefore never witnessed angry domestic fights. I considered myself to be a loyal and faithful partner and I took pride in those qualities. The men in my life confused me with their erratic, unpredictable, narcissistic qualities and behavior. It took me years to realize this is typical of the cycle of abuse. I finally married at age thirty and thought I had broken the cycle. This reminds me of my friend Jackie, who had a similar situation.

A Toxic Place

About a dozen years and several children after her marriage, Jackie realized something needed to change. She began educating herself through the counsel and guidance of a friend who was a licensed and trained social worker. She also read two books: two she still recommends to friends and clients: *The Verbally Abusive Relationship* by Patricia Evans and *Freeing Yourself from the Narcissist in your Life* by Linda Martinez-Lewi. She went to the local crisis center. She discovered that a covert narcissist is a wolf in sheep's clothing; they lie, cheat, and manipulate to get what they want. Their ego is built to avoid shame and accountability. They are masters of deflection and projection, lack basic empathy for others, are chief masqueraders and manipulators, like to debate, and can be hostile and combative with a goal of winning at all costs. It took Jackie years to see these patterns; when she needed her husband most, he was furthest away. Believe me, it was a hard truth for her to face when she realized she was sleeping with the enemy. She had not only herself to consider, but the children who depended on her. Her home was no longer a safe harbor, if it had ever been.

Although my situation was different from Jackie's, the realization that my marriage was no longer working after thirteen years catapulted me into what I call my darker days. During this time, I had quite a vivid dream: I was in my backyard and saw a magnificent tree with interesting textures and patterns on its trunk and shimmering leaves on its branches. When I looked down at the tree's base, however, it was almost like a horror movie where the scary music starts. I saw that the tree just hovered above the ground. It had been hollowed and it was black inside, almost as if burned and charred. This was a haunting picture, to be sure, and one I can still draw up easily. It was then that I realized what it was reflecting to me: *I was not rooted in anything. I was untethered; I had lost connection with my very spirit and self.*

Knowledge was power, and I began to take my trampled spirit and life back; I needed to reclaim my lost soul and spirit. The time was now, and I simply could not, *would not*, continue and accept living in a marriage that was so badly aligned with my values, my sense of who I was and how I felt a relationship should be. I had reached my tipping point. It was time to act with courage and make big changes. I was worthy of more in life.

I set firm boundaries and was able to remove myself from what had essentially become a dysfunctional relationship. I asked for a divorce. I had some healing to do. In my private practice, I journaled and maintained a vigilant yoga practice. I meditated. I went to the river for walks and cried and prayed. I also picked up an acoustic guitar and began playing it, which also became a salve, an instant reprieve. These were painful yet extremely cathartic days. I just couldn't stop and curl up in a ball; my children needed me, and I needed me. I became empowered and stronger with each passing day, week, and month, and I acquired more strength and clarity.

Dreams inform and shed insight. To the clairvoyant or clairsentient, they can also foretell. But for most of us, it is precious information, so do not discount or discard them all. Some have great meaning. One dream I had, as I was divorcing my husband, carried insight for me. We had finalized most of the particulars about our split, the division of assets, the visitation and joint custody schedules with the children, etc. I had decided to move from our marital home and rent a house closer to my daughter's school. I needed a change. I realized when I woke up that this vivid dream was such a metaphor for what was happening in my life at the time...

I was outside in my painting class and there was a pile of rocks near me. Hidden amongst them—coiled, camouflaged, and poisonous—were a number of copperhead snakes. I tried to warn the others when I spotted them. I said, "I need a hatchet, a saw, a hammer." I wanted to rid us of this danger before anyone was bitten. At that time, someone kicked something onto me, and it was indeed a snake. It sank its teeth deep into my back and spine. There it was attached like a remora, like a bloodsucking leech, draining me of my life force. In a clear and quick act, without question in my mind, I reached behind me and pulled. The venomous viper's fangs ripped my flesh as I pulled hard, revealing an open wound. I was taken to the hospital by a few friends and on the way, slowly losing consciousness, I told my driver to call ahead to the hospital and get them to prepare the anti-venom antidote, time was of the essence. I was taken to the small Chevy Chase hospital in Maryland, which resembled a home with plants and pillows, and I knew I was safe from my enemy forces. He—my ex—was not there, in any way, shape, or form. I was free from him at last. That final and lasting purge, the extrication of the serpent, meant I was liberated and unshackled, not bound any longer, the truest antidote.

I know now (hindsight is close to 20/20) that this was my recovery stage, the place to do most of my healing, my safe house, a half-way house as it were. I was not in my marital home anymore, away from old and toxic memories, renting temporarily until my youngest daughter graduated from high school.

I emerge, five years later, the old and often-used chrysalis metaphor indeed still applying. I have packed up and moved on to a new house and home—a clean slate. With my daughter headed off to college, I am an official empty nester. That era, my life in Maryland, is complete. I moved away from the old life, the one that holds both joy and sorrow. The two are inextricably wound within it; one cannot separate the two, *and that is life*! Most assuredly the way we process, heal, and grow from the challenges and events that life hits us with is what counts. And so, I emerge, as I hope you do, too, with greater clarity than I have known before, my life's calling and the path cleared now, unobstructed. I am counting my blessings.

Inspiration for Today:

Keep a dream log when you have an impressionable dream. It can give you insights and affirmations in a world where we doubt ourselves. Egyptian, Mesopotamian, Greek, Mayan, Peruvian, Hebrew, and Native American cultures, to name a few, believed in the importance and power of having prophetic dreams.

ON HARBORING
ANGER AND HATE

*What do sad people have in common? It seems
they have all built a shrine to the past and often go
there to wail and worship. What is the beginning of
happiness? It is to stop being so religious like that.*

—Hafiz

I t distresses me to see anger and vitriol fill people's
hearts. It does not serve us, not one bit. It's important in the healing path to surround ourselves with
like-minded people who are loving and supportive
and whose intentions are similar to our own. If there
is toxicity in your life, the sooner you identify it and
work to create healthy boundaries around the person
who delivers it, the sooner you will be free to heal. This
is also true for our own limiting beliefs, negative talk
and self-doubts, and any thoughts of low self-worth.
Do you know how incredibly amazing you are?

Inspiration for Today:

Thus, in the spirit of being kinder to yourself, I offer this story and suggest this practice:

I was once ordering a pendant for a necklace, treating myself to a moderately priced piece of jewelry for my birthday. The order form asked me if this was a gift. I was about to type "no." Then I paused and typed, "yes," and thought, "yes, this is a gift to me, from me." And this was what I wrote in the gift message of the card: *"You are a marvelous, luminous, magical spirit and soul, and we are all lucky to have you in this world."* When it arrived in my mailbox, I smiled big!

THE IMPORTANCE
OF FORGIVENESS

*Forgiving is holiness; by forgiveness, the Universe
is held together. Forgiveness is the might of the
mighty. Forgiveness is sacrifice; forgiveness is
quiet of the mind. Forgiveness and gentleness
are the qualities of the self-possessed.*

—The Mahabharata

F orgiving yourself and others is essential to healing your whole self. And I will add that the process simply cannot be sped up. It takes time. Ask yourself, "How much hate do I have in my heart?" This can be for a former partner, a relative, a boss, a co-worker, or a political leader. Know that it does not serve you, not one bit. If there is toxicity in your life, the sooner you identify it and work to create healthy boundaries with that person, situation, or memory, the sooner you will be free to heal.

A Mythological Story

Once there was a woman who lost her purpose in life. She was far, far from the place she knew she was meant to be. She had been born with this knowledge but had somehow lost it as she had grown older. Her early life had been a garden of beauty. She had love and laughter and a clear mind that was able to appreciate these good and wondrous things. She saw beauty everywhere in people, animals, the earth, the moon, and the stars. Sadly, she grew older and met a man who liked to think of himself as a great prince, a condor, an eagle—as strong as a bull and as fierce as a lion. While she still witnessed beauty, the joyous love in her heart began to fade; a light was dimming, disappearing.

The day came when the woman found herself broken and depleted of her very spirit; she was a shell of herself, and she walked in darkness. It was then that she heard the echoes and the whispers of the ancient sages, the great and gentle spirits who guide us, came to her, and said, "No, don't you see? He is not the great prince, condor, eagle, bull, or lion. It is you. You have all the traits that he longs for; you will draw on this courage and strength and you will clearly see one day, just as clearly as you did when you were young and held such purity in your heart and so much love for others—animals, your family, the earth, moon, and stars. You will one day regain and have this perspective again, only it will be sweeter, and you'll be stronger. And so upon hearing this, she climbed the mountain and sat still and understood. She sat in stillness and realized the beauty in herself and the world surrounding her, reveling in the awesome wonder here on Earth. And so it was, and so it is.

The End.

Inspiration for Today:

Be honest with yourself: Who do you need to forgive most in order to move on? Write a mythological story like the one above and speak in the third person; it can be a very good exercise and you may be surprised— your story may flow out quickly and just write itself.

THE IMPORTANCE
OF SEEKING HELP

An arrow can only be shot by pulling it backward, so
when life is dragging you back with difficulties,
it means that it's going to launch you into
something great. So just focus and keep aiming.

—Anonymous

Take the steps you can to heal yourself, but by all means, ask for help when you need it. There is no shame in asking for help. Find a professional therapist, medical doctor, energy worker, or healer. All can work in tandem, as well. The goal is to do the work and find the healing. If a professional operates with integrity, then something positive should follow. Seek medical assistance and also explore the world of alternative therapies—Reiki and intuitive healers, craniosacral therapists, acupuncturists, massage therapists—whatever works for you. It is a very personal decision. There are healing powers in all these modalities.

NCADV (National Coalition Against Domestic Violence) Facts:

- In the United States, more than 10 million adults experience domestic violence annually.
- 1 in 4 women and 1 in 9 men have experienced some form of physical violence, sexual abuse, or stalking by an intimate partner during their lifetime.
- On a typical day, domestic violence hotlines receive 19,000 calls.[***]

Domestic violence is prevalent in every community and affects all people regardless of age, socio-economic status, sexual orientation, gender, race, religion, or nationality. Domestic violence can result in physical injury, psychological trauma, and even death.

The Domestic Violence Victims Hotline

The Domestic Violence Victim's Handbook states that domestic violence is a pattern of coercive behavior

---

[***]National Coalition Against Domestic Violence (2020). "Domestic Violence." Retrieved from https://assets.speak-cdn.com/assets/2497/domestic_violence-2020080709350855.pdf?1596811079991. Accessed September 28, 2023.

characterized by the domination and control of one person over another, usually an intimate partner, through physical, psychological, verbal, sexual and/or economic abuse.

The Power and Control Wheel developed by the Domestic Abuse Intervention Project[****] (www.duluth-model.org) indicates that you are in an abusive relationship if your partner:

- puts you down
- berates you
- belittles you
- makes you feel bad about yourself
- calls you names
- makes you think you're crazy
- plays mind games
- makes you feel guilty
- uses male privilege
- makes all the big decisions
- uses children against you
- minimizes, denies, and blames you for things they did

[****]National Domestic Violence Hotline, "Power and Control" National Coalition Against Domestic Violence (2020). Domestic violence. Retrieved from www.hotline.org https://assets.speakcdn.com/assets/2497/domestic_violence-2020080709350855.pdf?1596811079991. Accessed September 28, 2023.

- makes light of the abuse
- does not take your concerns seriously
- says the abuse didn't happen
- says you caused them to behave abusively
- uses jealousy to justify their actions and
- controls what you do

Crisis Hotlines:

There are many resources available to individuals seeking help or hotlines. Know that there are professionals who are willing to help in crisis centers and by text or phone.

Here is a list of organizations within the US:

National Domestic Violence Hotline: Phone 1-800-799-SAFE (1-800-799-7233),
TTY: 1-800-787-3224

National Suicide Prevention Lifeline Phone
1-800-273-TALK
(1800-273-8255), TTY: 1-800-799-4889 or text #988

RAINN is the nation's largest anti-sexual violence organization. RAINN created and operates the National Sexual Assault Hotline in partnership with more than 1,000 local sexual assault service providers across the country.

National Sexual Assault Hotline (offering confidential 24/7 support): online.rainn.org or 1-800-656-4673

Dating Abuse: Love Is Respect is support specifically aimed at teen and young adult relationships. 1-866-331-9474, TTY: 1-866-331-8453 or Text LOVEIS to 22522

Book Recommendations:

The Verbally Abusive Relationship by Patricia Evans

Freeing Yourself from the Narcissist in your Life by Linda Martinez-Lewi

Stop the Silence, Thriving After Child Sexual Abuse by Dr. Pamela Pine, available on Amazon.

Inspiration for Today:

Help a friend in need! Please share hotline numbers with your friends or family members if they seem like they are struggling with something. With mental health illness statistics on the rise, there is no doubt someone you know is suffering. Reach out— you could be helping to save a life.

IN CONCLUSION

From a certain point onward
there is no longer any turning back.
That is the point that must be reached.

—Kafka

Know this: life gets messy, and the road is not straight. Nor would we want it to be. It is in the bends and jags that we can grow, optimize, and elevate ourselves to a newer, better, more meaningful way of being in life. We are given many opportunities along the way to learn, to grow, to stretch and expand into the very best version of ourselves. Not all of us will embrace and accept the invitation, this assignment, the task to do so. But if you do, then you undoubtedly are a seeker, seeking to expand upon and grow into the highest levels of your very self. And I say to you a heartfelt *Congratulations!* for heeding this call; the rewards will be many.

It is equally important to remember on this journey that you are not responsible for another person's happiness, your children included. They have their own access to wisdom and abundance, as do we. Also, it is important to remember that if you are a parent, your children have their own guides in life. Trust in this. Do not carry loved ones' burdens, worries, or weight for them. Worrying is not love. Yes, we are here to provide them with love and support and be a kind of guidepost, but it's essential to know and trust that they are on their own individual journeys, just as we are.

Despite these hardships and challenges I've suffered along the way, I am grateful for all my struggles because they have made me the person I am today; I am the sum of all these parts. I now have a peaceful serenity that comes after having fought a long and difficult battle and coming out the other side with a sense of real wholeness. I have found freedom and true joy, and I have experienced deep personal self-growth. My pain has been transmuted. I value and love myself and, most importantly, I have the courage to live and love again with an open heart.

We must not forget that we are magical beings on a magnificent journey. There are mysteries and miracles in our midst, extending out into the great beyond, some unexplainable and much of the time unquantifiable. It is not surprising when we learn, then, about our origins, our creation, that we were made from very elements of the stars themselves. The atoms in your body were created at the start of our universe during the Big Bang. So, if you look at it this way, you're about 13.7 billion years old. These atoms were created in the dying stage of an exploding star called a supernova. Therefore, it can be said that your body was forged inside a star that died. You are bits and pieces of star and cosmic dust! Carl Sagan and Neil deGrasse Tyson all espouse this. The top four ingredients in life and in your body are: hydrogen, oxygen, carbon, and nitrogen. These are also the very same chemically active atoms found in the universe. We are living on this beautiful planet full of life and, in a kind of genius symbiosis with our oceans and our forests, are breathing in the very oxygen the plants emit. Our bodies are marvels in and of themselves: our hearts beat involuntarily throughout the night while we dream and restore ourselves. Our five senses give us information, while our circulatory and cardiovascular systems, digestive and excretory systems, immune and lymphatic systems, integumentary and exocrine systems, respiratory and endocrine systems, are *all* at work in unison in one miraculous body.

And so it can also be said that our lives are tapestries woven from our own personal experiences of joys, sorrows, delights, and tragedies. We are here to experience it all—rising from our falls and continuing on despite the things that could so easily be our ruin and instead, learning from our experiences, growing wiser, developing clarity, and strength, moving through it all. I am a blend of the battle wounds and the scars all now fused, soldered, and repaired. You are, too. Remember that you can and will walk through the mire, having survived those circumstances, and be proud of the place in which you are currently standing.

I hope that you come to a clearing and discover a peaceful space and place to help you move forward into a new and healed part of your life, experiencing a kind of renewal—a reawakening. It is then that you will be able to focus on the next stage of your growth, of your personal development, your true life's purpose and calling. You are a gorgeous, radiant being of the Universe, illuminating God's love. May you find precious peace in your heart, and a quiet calm in your mind. Remember, there is infinite, great love surrounding you—it is in fact your very essence—and you are very worthy of receiving all of it.

I am not what happened to me;
I am what I choose to become.

- Carl Jung

INSPIRATION FOR TODAY NOTES:

_____

_____

_____

_____

_____

_____

_____

_____

_____

_____

_____

_____

_____

_____

_____

_____

_____

_____

_____

_____

_____

_____

_____

_____

_____

_____

_____

_____

_____

_____

_____

_____

_____

_____

_____

_____

_____

_____

_____

_____

_____

_____

_____

_____

_____

_____

_____

_____

_____

_____

_____

_____

_____

_____

_____

_____

_____

_____

_____

_____

_____

_____

_____

_____

_____

_____

_____

_____

ACKNOWLEDGMENTS

I would like to thank my teachers and instructors in the realm of healing and fine arts for giving me the tools I needed to navigate this world in my own way, so that I may bring healing to others and express through my hands, paint and paintbrush, the beauty that still exists on this planet. I would like to thank friends Melanie O'Brien and Molly Harrison for doing the first passes on editing this book. It has evolved and taken shape over the years, and you have been a part of this idea and venture. I would be remiss if I did not give un grand merci to friend Thom Middlebrook for his artistic counsel on this and so many of my other ideas and projects. A special thank you to Tyne for her patience, perseverance, and wonderful aesthetic eye.

I would like to thank my editor, Susan Crossman, for your expertise and direction in all my writing projects, for truly hearing my voice, and for your validation and encouragement. I was not aware of the true catharsis telling these stories would bring and just how empowering it would be—thank you for believing in me. Thank you also to Susie Schaefer and Lisa

Shrewsberry for offering further direction and creative solutions in assisting and pulling the whole endeavor across the finish line!

To my three precious children: Maya, Charley, and Tyne for the light you bring to this world, the unique and individual talents you each possess—you make me proud to be your mother every day. I hope you live each of your brilliant lives to the absolute fullest. Thank you for supporting me in my dreams of being an artist, a writer, and a healer, and for cheering me on all the way! You are my three greatest blessings.

ABOUT THE AUTHOR

Christy Young facilitates wellness retreats in Elbow Cay, a five-mile-long cay in the Abaco Islands of the Bahamas. Her offerings include private Reiki sessions and group guided meditations; she believes it is easier to disengage amidst the fresh ocean breeze and a constantly changing cloudscape above the sea. These natural elements are conducive to feelings of serenity and healing on a deeper level.

In New York City, Christy paints at Chelsea Classical Studios, using live models in a classroom setting. She draws much satisfaction from the companionship and comradery she finds among the artists' community there. Christy creates her art mostly in oils, painting a variety of subjects beyond the human figure, ranging from outdoor landscapes, coastal scenes, waterfalls, trees, florals, and still life. Her most important project is currently being developed in her home studio: a solo exhibition slated for 2025 in Richmond, Virginia.

While not working within the realms of Reiki, painting, or writing, Christy relishes time spent outdoors, scouting wildlife on the hiking trails of Great Falls, Maryland. She savors, too, the sensation of quietly gliding over calm waters on a paddleboard, held captive by the sights and sounds under the big sky above.

Christy can often be found in a gallery or museum gazing at the artwork on the walls and seeking artistic inspiration. Some of her fondest memories are of taking her three young children to the National Gallery of Art in Washington, D.C., where they would bring notecards, paper, and colored pencils to create their own works of art while studying their favorite pieces.

Christy supports live music, be it in a local tavern, an intimate jazz club in the city, or an outdoor music summer venue. She thoroughly enjoys the blissful moments she finds while practicing musical pieces on her Gretsch resonator and her Martin D-18. Christy's beloved cat, named after the jazz pianist Thelonious Monk, will sometimes sit on her stereo speaker, seemingly digging the vinyl collection which plays on the turn table alongside her.

She lived in Paris, France for two years and while there, nurtured a bona fide affinity for an authentic chocolate croissant from the corner boulangerie. She adores handwritten notes and letters, and delights in books of all kinds, especially the old-fashioned kind with paper, and particularly a well-crafted book of poetry. Look for her collected book of poems, coming out next year.

Christy inherited an appreciation for canning dilled beans from her Grandmother Olivia and finds pleasure in making a good batch of mason jars full and gifting to friends and family. Her next venture, or her "pie in the sky," is to expand her outdoor garden to grow additional vegetables and berry bushes. She remembers a large raspberry bush her family had for many years in the backyard growing up, and revels in the sweet memory of her mother making the most heavenly, unforgettable raspberry pie in the summertime that you've ever tasted.

Connect with Christy:
Instagram: @christyyoungartist
Website for Art: www.christyyoungfineart.com
Reiki & Energy Work: www.christyyoungwellness.com
Retreats: www.newmorningretreat.com